*This Pawesome Coloring Book
Belongs To:*

_____

_____

**MY HOUSE GOT ROBBED WHILE
I WAS SLEEPING.**

Daddy went fishing. I stole his catch while he was cleaning and hid it in the couch.

Sometimes I sleep in the laundry pile. Sometimes I pee in it.

I'm not fat.
I'm a little husky.

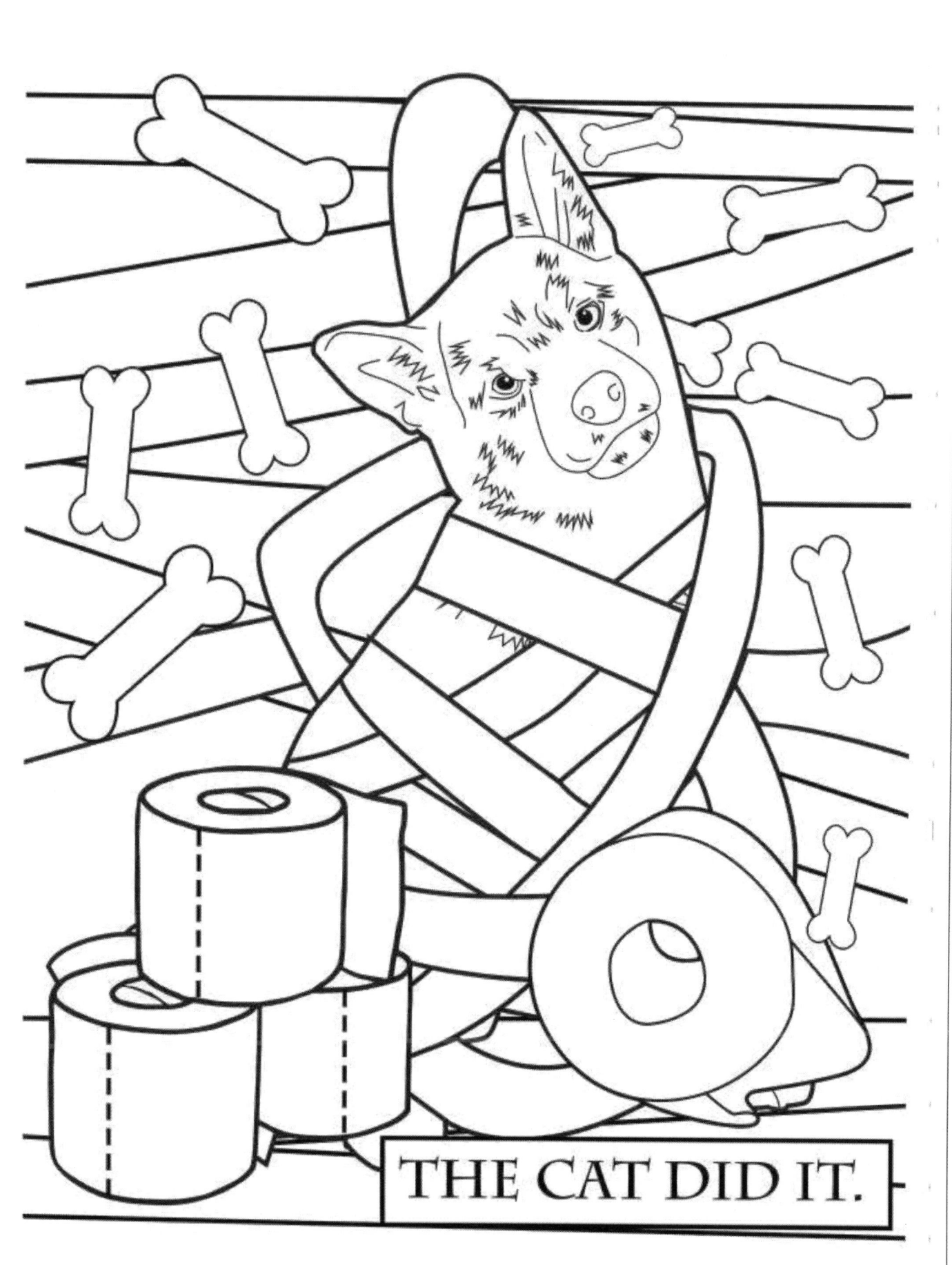

THE CAT DID IT.

I bark at the big dogs when mommy takes me for a walk. Then I hide behind mommy if they bark back.

I DON'T ALWAYS BARK BUT WHEN I DO IT'S IN THE MIDDLE OF THE NIGHT

I DIDN'T CHOOSE THE PUG LIFE.

THE PUG LIFE

CHOSE ME.

Printed in Great Britain
by Amazon